You Are Not Smaller Than the Room

By Temesghen Starr

You Are Not Smaller Than the Room © 2018 to Temesghen Starr

ISBN: 9781513643717

All rights reserved. Printed in the United States of America and Canada. No part of this book may be used or reproduced in any manner without written permission by the author, except in the case of brief quotations within critical articles or reviews.

Although the author and publisher have made every effort to ensure that the information in this book was correct at press time, the author and publisher do not assume and hereby disclaim any liability to any party due to these words coming from the author's own opinion based on their experiences. Some names have been changed to protect privacy.

This book is based on the author's own personal experience and their personal development journey. Although we have made every reasonable attempt to achieve complete accuracy in the content of this book, we assume no responsibility for errors or omissions in the information in this book.

You should use this information as you see fit and at your own risk. Your life and circumstances may not be suited to these examples the author shares within these pages. This book is intended to be a guide and is not a replacement for professional advice.

How you choose to use this information in this book within your life is completely your responsibility and risk.

Published by Follow It Thru Publishing:
http://followitthrupublishing.com/

Cover Design by Lorraine Shulba: https://www.bluebugstudios.com/

Editing by Jen Sabillon: http://theladybosscollective.com

Copyediting by Suzanne LaVoie:
https://www.suzannelavoiewrites.com/

Proofreading by Amanda: www.letsgetbooked.com

Formatting by Bojan Kratofil: https://www.expertformatting.com/

Table of Contents

Massively Propel Your Confidence One Step at a Time 1

Foreword 5

Blessing 8

Chapter 1: Learned Confidence 9

Chapter 2: Defining Moments 14

Chapter 3: Dreams + Confidence: Partners in Crime 23

Chapter 4: Nature vs. Nurture: What a Winning Culture Can Do for Your Life 28

Chapter 5: Losing and Gaining Confidence 39

Chapter 6: Fear of the Unknown 45

Chapter 7: Socioeconomics and Confidence 51

Chapter 8: Self-Love: The Foundation 57

About the Author 62

Massively Propel Your Confidence One Step at a Time

Preface: *You are not smaller than the room!*

Success and the measure of where we want to be stems from something very simple that we all have within us. It's something that is so uncomplicated, it almost makes you laugh when you hear this one simple word. This one word will tie so much of life together.

That word is **confidence**.

But it is not confidence in the sense of how one is acting; rather, it is more the essence of who one is. That being comes to us through situations, experiences, and beliefs that we have. Even more important than those times in our lives that have led us to this confidence is what we believe in ourselves to be true and the way that that confidence propels us.

Confidence is not just who we are; it is also what we outwardly project. Attitude and essence are what enter a room before our physical bodies ever do. This is our reputation.

This is who we are.

In life, we are all told to go out and achieve great things. We are taught that we need to go out and succeed. We are also taught that we need to work hard to get what we want.

However, no one ever told us the very elementary intangible that could help us achieve great success - some know this behavior to be the most important piece necessary to reach all these markers in the equation. What is that one simple ingredient that we always need? That ingredient that helps to propel us forward is **confidence.**

For those of us who have ever struggled with confidence, felt as though we were not good or important enough, this book is for **us.** How does confidence play a part in combating these feelings of unworthiness, less-than, or insignificance? That is what we will tackle together.

We will also touch on the different situations that lead us to think we are not as big as the room. Those moments when life makes us feel like the smallest speck on this planet with little to no seriousness whatsoever.

Finally, we will talk through some different tactics and address the ways in which we can inwardly protect our outward expression.

I came to an affinity with this topic, as I most recently changed career industries. I moved into a career that I was unfamiliar with, uncertain if I would be successful, and one that I was completely unsure of.

However, one thing I *did* know was that there were very successful people in my life in the industry. And those successful people did not have anything that was any different from what I had deep inside of me. At that particular moment, it set in for me that I *knew* confidence was one of the key driving factors in all of those people that were successful. I came to the realization that if I moved forward like the successful people before me, I only needed to bet on myself and the rest would follow.

That, in itself, takes confidence and the willingness to believe in yourself.

After having some immediate success in my new industry, I thought to myself, *Why were others not finding success, too?*

Again, that answer came back to confidence.

In sales, the person that can get the other individual sitting across the table to buy into what he/she is selling is the person that is in control. This person is usually one who is charming, witty, likable, and most importantly – *confident*. These attributes carry over into our personal lives, as well. All of this usually stems from experiences that we have carried in from our own unique paths.

As we take this journey to mastering confidence together, I want to help those who are new to sales, networking, lacking in confidence because of past experiences, and need a boost in confidence to realize that *they are not smaller than the room.*

If you only hear one thing throughout this entire book, I hope you hear this: **you are not smaller than any room.**

This book is intended for individuals who have recently had some relationship changes in their lives and keep feeling like they are missing something crucial, as if they are not good enough to be a part of that same social circle as before.

It's also for those who don't live in the same financial space as their peers, which makes them doubt their abilities and worth altogether.

This book will leave a mark for those who simply believe that they are not certain how confidence will propel them to new heights and aspirations that were previously set.

I want to touch the person who has all the tools but just does not have the belief. It is time for us to face our fears and embrace the power we have within to achieve.

And it all starts with **confidence**.

Foreword

"I am 100% confident in every situation, 100% of the time," said no one *ever*. Confidence. It's something we all want more of. We have all struggled with a lack of confidence at some point in our lives. As a psychologist and high-performance coach, I hear all too often how the absence of confidence prevents people from reaching their highest selves and achieving success.

So, what is confidence? How do we get more of it? Why do some people seem to have gobs of it, while others struggle to find it at all? Is it something a person is born with, or can it be learned?

The answers to those questions are exactly what this book aims to teach you.

In my opinion, confidence is simply **the belief in one's ability to figure things out**. The keyword here is *belief*. Our beliefs are the direct result of two things – the thoughts we think and the actions we take. The good news is that new research into neuroplasticity reveals that we can rewire our brains in ways that can positively change our thoughts and behaviors, at any age. What this means, then, is that it's never too late to become confident!

Thoughts and behaviors feed each other in a bidirectional way. In other words, you can think your way into different behaviors and behave your way into different thinking.

Let me give you an example. Let's say you have a big test to take, and you lack the confidence to earn a good grade. What can you do? You can study. Studying (the behavior) will change your thoughts *(I should do well on the test because I have prepared)*, leaving you feeling more confident about the upcoming test. Doing well on the test will change your thoughts about your future ability to be a good test-taker. I call this the **competence-confidence loop**. One of the best things you can do to increase your confidence is learning the skills necessary to work and maintain that behavior better and more skillfully.

As a psychologist, I think it needs to be said that sometimes *confidence can be highly overrated*. Let me explain. Sometimes we are challenged to do things that are important to us, and we have little to no confidence in our abilities at all. This is especially true for things we are trying for the first time. Our brains know the data and say to us, *You have no track record of success here. What do you think you're doing?*

In these situations, I would suggest that two strategies can be highly effective in growing one's confidence. The first is **borrowing someone else's confidence**. Years ago, I was training for my first bodybuilding competition. I had absolutely no confidence that my body could get into the shape I knew was necessary to not make a complete fool of myself on stage. I remember one day, wanting to quit, and crying in the weight room (not a good look). My trainer asked me, "Do you trust me? Do you have confidence in my ability to train you to be ready?" I did. I told her I had full faith in her, to which she replied, "Then borrow my belief until you get your own." I borrowed her confidence and placed my confidence in her abilities, not my own, to help me reach my goal. (I ended up winning four trophies, by the way, which you better believe helped grow my confidence.)

The second way to build confidence is practicing **being courageous**. Courage is not the absence of fear, but rather, the mastery of fear. When you stretch yourself outside of your comfort zone, you will reap the rewards of greater confidence.

In summary, these strategies are what I call the **3 C's of Confidence**:

1. **Competency:** Learn and practice the skills necessary to grow your confidence.

2. **Courage:** Step outside of your comfort zone to increase your confidence.

3. **Connection:** Borrow someone else's belief or look to their example of success and apply it to your situation.

Get ready to dive into this book and learn even more strategies to grow your confidence. And before you do, ask yourself, *Haven't I been through enough? Can't I see that I have a great track record of figuring things out?* You do. You really do. I'm confident about that.

Repeat after me, *Everything is figure-out-a-ble.*

Confidently yours,
Dr. Erin

Blessing

Loving my children has always pushed me in ways I often didn't see coming or have not recognized until graced with moments to stop and reflect.

Any relationship of value requires courage: courage shaped by what each relationship needs.

Each one of us will find ourselves defining—sometimes by the simplest of actions—the kind and quality of confidence that will express the love that moves and motivates our being and our doing.

This book is one of those grace moments. I'm pushed to be clear for myself in a fresh definition of confidence. A definition I can share with my children as they shape their own for a generation waiting and hungry to learn.

Confidence is the living courage to trust the wisdom of recognizing that hard and strong are not the same thing, and knowing from one moment to the next which of these is the better servant.

Rev. Dr. Albert Starr Jr.

Chapter 1

Learned Confidence

Early Childhood and Confidence

As a young child, I was always valued and listened to—with the best intentions—the adults in my life.

The things that I was good at and took an interest in were constantly encouraged by the adult figures in my life. They pushed me to do better, be better.

As a child, I knew how good it felt to have support from the adults I cared for the most in my life. I started believing what they were saying and could see the happiness exude from within myself, as well as from the adults in my life, when I mastered something new.

I felt confident in my abilities because those around me were confident in me *and* in themselves.

So, is it pretty safe to assume that confidence starts as a child?

I would most definitely agree with that statement.

Confidence is a behavior that children learn and receive from the very beginnings of their upbringing. Childhood couldn't be more of a pivotal point for creating confidence in a person.

This is a characteristic that is delivered to each child from the adults they are surrounded by and influenced by daily.

Young children are told to be proud of who they are and mimic the behavior of those people that care most about them. It is quite easy, in fact, to see that children who are exposed to a large number of proud, confident adults in their lives exude the same behavior.

And they continue to shine with exuberant confidence throughout their entire lives.

If a child is fortunate enough to be given the opportunity by adults in his or her life to have big visions and grand situations that call for confidence, that same minor will continue to use this character trait to propel through life.

Even though I received that kind of support and encouragement in my life as a young child, it couldn't stop there. As adults, the support had to continue throughout my entire life and spill into every part of my life.

It couldn't just be about the sports I was mastering or the skills I was acquiring; this confidence had to extend into *every facet* of my life from those same adults.

As a parent, I work on this on a daily basis. My son and I sit nightly working on his reading (a summertime exercise he doesn't always look forward to).

I've always tried to support him and provide massive confidence in every area of his life, especially learning.

When I sit down to read with my son, I sometimes have to remind him that embracing the time we spend together reading should be similar to the time he loves playing soccer together.

While soccer is definitely his happy time (and what kid doesn't love playing outside), he enjoys it mostly because he's really good at it.

He's good at most sports he plays, and he really loves competition. That is the time when his cup is full and his confidence overflows.

However, reading is a bit more of a challenge for him. At first, when we started our nightly reading routine, he did not jump at the opportunity. I didn't fault him for that.

After we had a talk about practice and the time it takes to really get good at something, he was much more accepting of the idea. He started liking the time spent on reading when he became more confident in his reading abilities.

When you can show children that the confidence within everything about them is something that they *can* master, they believe it! They embrace that it is not something that just happens but that it will actually take effect and help them become a bit more of a master at the sill.

Having the opportunity to have supportive talks with my son allows me to leave indelible marks that create confidence for future situations no matter what he's facing.

That is exactly what the adults in my life have always shown me. They supported me and allowed me to feel like I could do anything. And if there was something I couldn't do, they left the space open for me to come and talk about it with them.

There was not one thing that I didn't feel I could tackle with or without their help.

Adults in my life always showed me a great deal of support, and because of that support, I felt my village surrounding me at all times.

You Are Not Smaller Than the Room

This wasn't only because I was a cute kid, but rather due to my speaking with conviction about the things that I was passionate about because I felt confident in my abilities.

At the tender age of four, I vividly remember inviting all of the adults in my life to a basketball game that was to be held at my school. Is this a big deal or anything out of the ordinary? Not particularly.

I did play basketball at the YMCA, and the adults would always come to my games to show their support.

However, this game was different. This was not just another basketball game at the preschool.

This game was bigger than that.

I remember the intricate planning and other details from memories retold by those adults I invited. Throughout all of the memories and stories I have been told, one thing was rooted in all of it: there were deep confidence boosters infused throughout the entire situation.

As I remember it, this was the game of all games. All the kindergarteners were playing against the pre-kindergarteners. This was certainly going to rival the Showtime Lakers in 1987 - there was no doubt.

Of course we needed concessions, and my Aunt Karen was set to handle that.

We needed a referee, so Uncle Raymond stepped up to handle that.

Most importantly, we needed someone to keep score. Mom and Dad would suffice for this duty.

The game was happening on Friday afternoon after lunch because that's when big afternoon playtime was around those parts.

When we all think back on this game, everyone gets a kick out of it because of the seriousness that was involved in the planning. I was not playing games (other than the basketball game).

Everyone played their part, even Uncle Raymond who showed up with a referee shirt and some hot dogs for the concession stand. We're not completely positive he didn't know this was just a scheme I had cooked up in my head.

To this day, we all get a good laugh at the story.

Of course, my parents had to give me a talking to about imagination and how it affects lives (not just ours but others' as well).

But one thing my family did not do was tell me that the basketball game couldn't happen the way I had envisioned it.

This game helped me to believe and be confident in the fact that I, too, still have the support of them. And I knew that I could always do an event and have support when the proper planning is in place.

And this one instance created more confidence in my little four-year-old mind than most knew was possible, and I have continued to carry that confidence with me throughout my entire life.

Here's to more 4-year-old basketball games with hot dogs and referees at the big afternoon playtime showdown.

Chapter 2

Defining Moments

Looking back on my life, I can honestly say that the riveting four-year-olds vs. five-year-olds recess basketball games were some of the most defining moments of my entire life. It may sound kind of crazy to you, but that was a moment in my life that built me up without me even realizing it.

I'm sure there have been times in your life that you have looked back on and thought, *Wow, that was life changing!* But in that very moment, you probably did not recognize it for what it was worth. In fact, most of us downplay those moments more often than we appreciate them when they are happening in real time. As the old saying goes, hindsight is always 20/20.

Take a journey with me. Stop and reflect on your life for a moment; think back on those monumental moments in your life. Can you pinpoint one that you truly feel deep down in your core defined who you were or were going to be? Maybe this is a positive or negative defining moment. There is no right or wrong answer here.

Of course you can. If I were a betting man, I'd bet you came up with two or three occasions in your life that you feel defined you either in a good way or a bad way. Those are the moments that shape us into who we are today.

What is crucial to remember is that our confidence was shaped the exact same way.

Much like my preschool basketball game, your confidence is shaped by experiences and influences that surround you throughout your life. Some of those influences and experiences weren't in your life by choice - they were given to you by design from a higher being.

Either way, you have been exposed to some monumental times that have helped create the confidence you now possess.

You may find yourself with a great deal of confidence—unafraid to speak in front of a large crowd, willing to assert your opinions into tough conversations, confident in your ability to do your job well, and so forth.

Or, you may find yourself struggling to get a true grip on your confidence—where a large group of people makes you feel uncomfortable, you're unsure of your contributions to your current job, and you don't pursue your dreams because you're too afraid you might fail.

Even though the basketball games occurred when I was just a young boy, I remember much of what made those moments so vital to who I am today. I know one thing for certain: my dreams and visions were always fueled by other people's confidence in me. In turn, their confidence evolved into my own confidence.

This happens to everyone, whether we realize it or not.

When we are young children, we don't fully grasp the concept that certain people's beliefs about us shape us into the adults that we become. Of course, we have the free will to choose who we want to be, but when it boils down to it, your actions, as well as your future, self-reflect what your past self-received and perceived from others.

It's time we take it all the way back to the very basics of what we perceived as confidence when we were young children.

Any kid will tell you that learning how to read is the most exciting thing they've ever done. The fire inside of them is so bright, and their hunger to learn more words is truly insatiable. That fire is there is until they face hardships with reading and refuse to try reading again due to too many failed attempts.

What makes that one kid decide to move past the failures and work on what they know they must learn? Where is the disconnect between the child who pushed forward and the child who stayed behind?

It's quite simple, actually. The answer is confidence received from other adults. Let's look at an example.

As a young child, I'm sure you remember your teacher giving everyone the chance to read aloud to the rest of the class. Every time the teacher would call on you for your turn, your heart fluttered, and your mind raced. Sometimes those flutters and mind racing were from excitement, and sometimes they were from sheer panic.

All it really took for you to feel confident that you could read aloud was the encouragement from your teacher and maybe even your peers. Even something as simplistic as, "You can do it, Bobby," got you through the fear and over to the other side.

It was those five small words that boosted your confidence and gave you the undeniable pleasure of knowing that you could, in fact, read aloud to the class and do an awesome job at it.

This is where the confidence from the influences in our lives comes from—that moment in your elementary school class where your teacher showed confidence in your abilities to read. That was all it took to deposit a small amount of confidence into your confidence bank. And those are the small deposits that ended up making your confidence what it is today.

***

If you've ever been around a pastor in your church or out in the community, you know that they have some serious confidence. In order to get up every Sunday morning and stand behind the pulpit, these pastors must embody great courage and confidence that many other professions do not require. In my eyes, pastors radiate a powerful confidence that shines down on their entire congregation. Their apparent belief in their abilities to share the word of God is what makes the rest of the congregation trust and lean into what they're saying on a weekly basis.

Luckily, I grew up with one of those incredibly confident pastors in my home. I called him Dad.

As you can imagine, growing up in a household where your father was a pastor meant you were held to a higher standard than most. I don't look back on those years and feel the oppression of the higher standards. What I do remember is how my father's confidence made me feel.

In grade school, there was a project assigned to the entire school. We all had to memorize a speech and recite it at school for a competition. Once the initial round of speeches were given, I was chosen as the representative speaker from my class. I competed with the memorized speech and won a showmanship award.

On the one hand, I know my father's influence as a pastor on my early childhood years had something to do with the confidence I felt in reciting my speech. But on the other hand, I also felt confident and proud of myself for memorizing a speech that not many other people can say they can do.

It truly was an experience that took what I was good at and boosted my confidence even higher. I was able to say, "I can do this."

I had someone in my life who exhibited incredible confidence, so I was able to see an example in my household every day of someone who was sure of his abilities. I was then able to harness that confidence and return it to the world in the form of believing in myself to get done what needed to be done.

You can feel that, too.

It might seem like a difficult thing to bring into your life now that you're older and the influential piece from your childhood has slipped away.

The truth of the matter is that your dreams and visions as a young child were fueled by the confidence you took on from those around you. You either went for your dreams because you knew you could do whatever you put your mind to thanks to the great people who instilled confidence in you, or you let those dreams and visions slip away because your influences didn't build you up and show you what you were able to do if you tried.

The good news is you are an adult who can make changes in your life right now.

It's okay if you didn't have X, Y, and Z like your friend Susan had. There are times in life when the losses cultivate our gains in the future.

My days as a foursquare athlete may have been long ago, but they still sit in my mind like they just happened yesterday.

There were more times than not in the earlier years of my foursquare playing days where I lost. I could have taken those losses and used them as my excuse to not have much confidence. I could tell myself that because I lost, I was not a good athlete. Maybe I could have even told myself I wasn't good at anything because I couldn't win a foursquare game.

As an adult, we are able to distinguish how ridiculous that sounds. If your child ever spoke those words to you, you would straighten them out and assure them that losing foursquare did not mean they weren't good at anything.

Those losses may have affected your confidence for a small time, and that's normal. They affected me because I was only a child. However, I was able to use those losses to remind myself that some things don't come so easily to me, and some things do. There may be some great foursquare players out there that struggle with the things I am great at doing.

There is always balance, and when you can take the losses you had when you were younger and turn them into opportunities to learn and grow from as an adult, you will see a shift in your confidence that may have seemed lost forever.

You are not tied to what your childhood gave you. Create your own story and let your confidence rise up from within from the incredible things you have done since those earlier years.

***

Confidence is never a one-shot deal. You don't have to live your life with little confidence simply because your situation dictated that for you in your early childhood years.

Living out your dreams and seeing visions for your life come to fruition can happen. There is nothing stopping you from harnessing new confidence and putting it out into the world as an adult.

In fact, finding that confidence from within as an adult can help shape the future confidences of those small children around you now.

The number one thing that has allowed me to channel my confidence since I was a young kid is the fact that I had adults in my life who supported me, but also kept me living in reality.

You can be that for a child, too.

You can be the influence that shows a child what confidence looks like.

No one ever told me I couldn't do something. Everyone in my life allowed me to dream and to look at my future self in any way I wanted to. They never held me back. I never held myself back.

It's time for you to step into your role as the influence and the impact on those children in your lives whether they are your own children, nieces, and nephews, students, or family friends. It is your responsibility to use your own experiences and confidence to support those children in your life.

One way adults can do this to teach the younger generation what confidence means. Show them that using words like "can't" are not helpful and productive; rather, they can replace them with words such as "can," which is empowering.

It's vital to not only tell kids they can do something, but also *show them* how to actually make it happen. Help them create the path that will help with achieving their dreams and goals. This is where they learn the confidence from—your support and their ability to accomplish the tasks it takes to achieve their goals.

A child simply needs to feel supported in order to feel confident. Tell them they are capable of reaching their goals and aspirations by helping them see the bigger picture.

It's easy for us as adults to question the dreams and ideas of children. After all, we know the logistics of achieving certain things, right? We know what will work and won't work. And oftentimes, we try to tell our children these logical thoughts because we think we're helping them. In reality, we're stifling their dreams instead of helping them figure out a plan to make it happen.

Even if they don't achieve what they were going for, they will still feel confident because you believed in them. Adults have the job of helping children see what is possible and helping them attempt to get to their end goal, regardless of the actual outcome.

***

Maybe your childhood was full of confident and influential people who have helped to shape you into a confident, powerful adult. And maybe your childhood couldn't have been further from that truth.

Whatever your childhood may have presented you with, remember these two things:

1. You have the ability to reshape your confidence into the powerful tool you want it to be.

2. It is your responsibility as an adult to help shape the confidence of those children in your life, so they can experience either what you did or something better.

You are in control of your confidence now. No one has the power over that part of your life—good, bad, or indifferent.

Chapter 3

Dreams + Confidence: Partners in Crime

We all have dreams for our lives - some dreams we know are more far-fetched than others, while some dreams are right within our reach.

After college, I was a high-school teacher with a dream of being a basketball coach. My first job led me to a head boys' basketball coaching position at South Bay Lutheran High-School. While I loved my job, I had dreams for a bigger opportunity.

I transitioned into a larger coaching role at a school with more students and more talent. This was what I had envisioned for myself - the opportunity to do something with a bigger scope.

The thing is, I reached my goal inadvertently just by becoming the head coach of a high-school basketball team at a very young age.

I also sought out something a little bit bigger for myself. Because I had previous experience as a high-level assistant coach, I believed in my abilities to do more and achieve more because I knew what it meant and took to be a coach to a team. My hunger to learn more about being a coach during my time as an assistant coach helped me grow confident in my abilities to later become a head leader of the team.

Knowing what I brought to the table was enough for me to know that I was the person for the position because I believed in myself and my abilities. That confidence came through in my life because I had previously achieved some level of success in that area of my life and knew that I could make it happen again.

In our lives, we experience different times where our status, accomplishments, and ability to achieve desired results helps us to encourage ourselves that we can do whatever we want at the next level. Any time we can prove to *ourselves* that we have the capabilities to do what we envision, we can then fully understand that we're eligible for those opportunities whenever they arise.

When it comes to dreams and confidence, I truly believe they are partners in crime. When we have something that is attainable and something we want to go after and achieve, there must also be a reason we want it all to happen.

Dreams have a great deal to do with confidence.

We simply have to hold something that is attainable and something that we want to go out and achieve to give us a reason to want to do certain things.

Dreams give us something to shoot for and reaching a seemingly unattainable landmark in our lives that lets us know we've officially made it.

Dreams give us that self-satisfaction to realize that we can, in fact, achieve certain heights. They help us see that we can achieve what we originally set out with our minds to do and that we can ultimately believe in ourselves to get these things done. All those confidence boosters can make us more self-assured people.

There is something that happens to our confidence when we're able to say, "YES, I did this, and I can do something else because I have accomplished something that I can always look back upon and be proud of."

Obstacles may arise, which can make achieving your dreams more difficult. But once you can get through those obstacles and accomplish what you want to achieve, those dreams will become a reality. This process builds upon the character and the foundation of what it is that we've had and what it is that we want to get. That, in turn, makes us more confident.

When I went for the high-school basketball coaching position, I knew that I had the ability to do what I really wanted to do.

I then took what I knew after my experience as a high-school basketball coach for a couple of years and the relationships I had formed with other coaches on club teams to get myself to the forefront of the program. There I was, with Los Angeles prospects, turning my dreams into realities with opportunities.

Ultimately, my dreams and visions in my mind of being a Division 1 college basketball coach were attainable because I knew had what it took to get there. My confidence was boosted because I knew what I brought to the table for those young boys and men from Los Angeles (and beyond).

It became clear to me that my background and network that I had built in the Los Angeles area had helped me form relationships that got me into other opportunities in the basketball community. I knew that coaches at the college level needed to be high caliber recruiters who knew how to pick talent and coach them.

This was where my confidence was greatly boosted. The thing is, we know that in order to achieve our dreams, we have to find connections in our lives that help us use our confidence to further ourselves.

Connecting with not only the players but also the specific program in which you work with is what makes a good coach. Being a recruiter for that program helps you embody confidence. In order to feel comfortable with yourself going out and looking for the best talent in the area can help you in other life situations, as well.

Let's face it—we can't all be the top dog all the time. However, you can be the person who uses their confidence and their knowledge of their skill sets to allow you to bring forth the confidence you needed to achieve greater things. Your confidence is your selling your point, and it is how you will close any deal.

I achieved my goals and saw my dreams become a reality using my confidence.

Not only was I a Division 1 basketball coach, but I was also hired into a program that I had sought after for quite some time, and I did this all by the age of twenty-five. I had achieved my goals and dreams because I was confident in the fact that what I was, who I was, and what I brought to the table was enough for an assistant coach position after two years.

I was hired at Montana State University as an assistant basketball coach—I had fulfilled my dream and my goal based on the confidence that I had within myself.

There is no doubt in my mind that I got where I wanted to go by setting goals based on my dreams and using confidence to get me to the end goal.

Why is that? Because I accept that when we believe in ourselves, we are able to move on to those goals in every different situation we're faced with.

It's safe to say that there may be people you don't believe you measure up to. And there are plenty of people on this planet who believe you shouldn't even measure yourself against others.

I'm not one of those people. In fact, I believe you should measure yourself against others for the simple fact that it gives you a good example of what it is you can achieve.

You can choose to say that Tom is no different than you and that you have all the same tools as Tom to get where you want to go. Tom, just like yourself, has everything he needs to be successful—and so do you.

Everyone has the ability to experience self-confidence. Everyone has the same twenty-four hours in a day.

The only difference is what dreams you have. What is that you want for yourself, and what do you want for the situation that is going to allow you to either succeed or not?

Chapter 4

Nature vs. Nurture: What a Winning Culture Can Do for Your Life

When I was hired at Montana State as an assistant basketball coach, I did not know the head coach very well at all. There was only a small chance to meet the head coach during general recruiting. We were busy recruiting players that had played at the junior college level and left ourselves very little time to get to know each other.

But what I was sure of was my ability to relate to kids from Southern California and actually get kids to come to Montana State from Southern California. There was no doubt in my mind that the best person for that particular job and that specific area was me. Who else could relate to those kids better than someone who had coached and lived there? Who better than someone who was actually from Los Angeles?

I knew that my abilities as a confident speaker, a person who could adapt easily, and a person who could easily fit into different situations when needed would get me where I needed to go with those kids the university so desperately wanted on their basketball team.

I believe that this situation boils down to one thing: confidence.

There is an undeniable fact about people who can walk into a room and know that they are skilled and able to complete the task at hand: they are confident in themselves.

These people aren't intimidated by those who are coming in the doors with them. They aren't intimidated by the financial statuses that are surrounding them. They aren't intimidated by the diverse situations that arise in a mixed room.

If this is who you aspire to be, someone who is *bigger* than the room itself and not the other way around, you have to be able to look at yourself and say, "I am confident, even if I'm walking into a room full of cool, and I'm just a bit goofy."

People will believe in you when you believe in yourself.

That confidence you have deep down inside of you should shine for the entire world to see.

That's what I did when I took the job at Montana State University. I knew that the situation was different—I was around different people in an unfamiliar place. But I knew my abilities were strong, and I could do what needed to be done. That's when people started believing in me as much as I believe in myself.

I didn't get there on my own, though. In fact, confidence has a great deal to do with nature rather than nurture. And I was able to go into that university and get the assistant coaching position because I had been nurtured throughout my life by some very influential people to believe in myself no matter what.

It may be difficult for you to find confidence. The life you had growing up may not have been the most conducive to nurturing your confidence, but that does not have to define you.

The environment that a kid grows up in has a great deal to do with their confidence—sometimes for the good and sometimes for the bad.

If kids do not see any sort of positive influence in their lives that shows them what confidence looks like, they will grow up without the understanding of what confidence truly means.

Think back on your childhood for a moment. Did you find yourself bouncing from multiple homes, schools, and circles of friends? Did you feel out of your element most of the time? Or did you have security, stability, and reassurance that whatever you wanted to do could be achieved because you had the capabilities and means to see success?

The nature of your surroundings would have dictated how you saw yourself and confidence from the very start.

Growing up in an area that did not support you and your dreams could've made you feel hopeless. But maybe there was something or someone who nurtured your confidence into what it eventually became.

Teachers, family, coaches, friends, and even employers can nurture our confidence and lead us to believe that we can do whatever we want to do in life. They helped you get to the point in your life that helped you see that you could reach whatever goals you set for yourself.

Support systems are the nurture to your nature—they are the loving communities that stand behind you every step of the way, regardless of your natural surroundings, to help breed confidence inside of you at all-time highs.

A child's environment can influence their confidence.

Research shows that children's environments shape how they will grow into adults. For example, home environments are credited for teaching children about how to act in certain situations. A child's environment is also responsible for shaping young ones' personalities and behaviors, both of which are closely linked to confidence.

Growing up, seeing parents who were consistently confident is what taught us to be confident within ourselves. That older brother of yours who was down in the dumps and didn't believe in himself at all let the other environmental elements surrounding him overshadow the incredible confidence your parents had.

This happens when the environment that surrounds us outside of the home is toxic and breeds negativity.

When kids are never taught that they can do anything besides what they're currently doing because of the negativity in their environment, including but not limited to the adults they interact with on a daily basis, they are unable to see what they *can* do.

You may have experienced an upbringing like this during your childhood. Maybe you heard those adults tell you you'd never be anything or go anywhere because of X, Y, Z. Or maybe those adults in your life that were meant to be support systems told you how you'd never be any better than they were.

Unfortunately, what happens in those situations is the adults don't want to see their children have any success in life if they don't get to experience it first. This belief also causes adults to force upon the child the idea that nothing is owed to that child and nothing great could possibly come from those concrete cracks.

The environment in this situation breeds the negativity and lack of self-confidence that many adults face well after childhood is over. Because living a life day in and day out full of uncertainty and negativity eventually leads one to believe the ideas that their adult influencers instilled in them (right or wrong). Imagine for a second that you were that child hearing all this daily. The sky would never be the limit for you. Instead, the stop sign down the street would be the only place you'd ever go.

On the flip side of things, when a child is given the opportunity to dream and look at big visions for their lives - those big, hairy, audacious dreams—they use the support system they have around them to achieve anything and everything they ever wanted.

When a child's environment shows them that confidence is there to tear down fear walls and build up their beliefs that they *can* do anything, no limits and no lids are placed on that child. They are able to see blue skies and sunshine ahead of them with a house on top of that hill. These children are able to desire these things because an adult along the way drove them by that house and said, "This is something that you *can* have. That house can be yours one day, no matter what your current circumstances may say, because the man inside that house right now didn't always have that house."

That is how confidence is built up in a child—the mere spoken word that that child can have whatever they want if they put their mind to it.

Winning Culture

You may have heard of the term *winning culture* before, or maybe it's a new term for you.

Either way, winning cultures are what makes or breaks a child from the start.

What exactly does it mean to have a winning culture, you may be asking yourself. That's a great question.

As with many definitions, some may hold differing opinions regarding what it takes to have a winning culture. For me, a winning culture means having set guidelines that an individual or team members use to believe in themselves and their abilities to break through any sort of goal blocker and reach any height they want to.

In a winning culture, you will find people spending a great deal of time training for what they want - athletics, academics, artistry, etc. They fight for what they want and believe they can actually win.

Having a winning culture puts forth a set of ideas based off of previous small successes in our lives that force us to believe that the next new obstacle, the next big game. The next activity is *ours* for the triumph because we are used to *winning* every battle that is put in front of us.

When a child is placed in an environment that encourages a winning culture, a child's mindset can be positively affected early on.

Growing up in the '80's in Southern California meant that I grew up watching the Showtime Lakers (my favorite basketball team). Deep down I know that I liked The Lakers for more than one reason.

Of course, I liked them because I was from California. The loyalty never dies for your home state athletic team. But I also found myself liking them as a team because those guys had fun when they played. I started to truly believe that basketball was always supposed to be a fun game because you were supposed to *win*.

I know that I thought this was the case because I had some amazing coaches along the way. John Slaven, my coach during my early years from five to eight years old, taught me that you can't always win every game. In fact, you won't always succeed, and you should always go into every game (and every situation) believing that you *can* win because you worked hard. You practiced, learned your opponent, done everything you possibly could, and connected with your team.

You not only believed in yourself but also your team. That winning culture that created a mindset of winning went into every game, every season, and every tournament.

Having set mindsets surrounding a winning attitude and culture allows you to really grow up believing that you *are* a winner. When you believe that you can win, and you enjoy the game at the same time, you've already won in the long run.

Of course you could measure your enjoyment or happiness on whether you won the game or not, but that wouldn't make much logical sense. At the end of the day, you have to be able to take the small wins before worrying about the big ones. Nothing about being proud of yourself, despite winning or losing, should be a disappointment or embarrassment.

One thing I've always tried to do—and I know it would benefit you as well—is break down the proverbial game into quarters, halves, teaching points, etc. This makes the fact that last game your team allowed your opponents to score twenty-five points on us in the first half of the game a teaching point that you can go back and tell yourself that you're going to reduce that number of allowed points. This is simply a reframing method that gives you a chance to look at a more positive spin on the loss.

Let's look at this example from a child's perspective.

If you're looking to increase the winning culture in your child's environment, you could take this opportunity (whether it's a basketball game or a math test) to enforce the idea that even if your child doesn't get the desired results the first time—they lose a game or don't score as highly on a test as they had hoped—they can still improve the next time around.

Nothing should be presented as an all-out loss. Instead, give your child something to look forward to—improving and boosting their confidence so they learn that they *can* improve. These are invaluable teaching moments that will stick with them for a lifetime.

Back in chapter 3, I talked about the wins that I experienced as a basketball coach. Moving up the ladder from a high-school coach to a junior college coaching position all the way up to a Division 1 coach was my win. That was my short-term goal. And for me, those wins proved that even though I didn't get to my top goal from the very start, I was still winning with each step I took toward the ultimate goal.

During the summer of 2016, I found myself within the first five months of being with a new company. Prior to that time, I came into the company at the tail end of February 2016 as a new agent. Throughout the next five months, I was able to move up through the company and become a producer that allowed me the opportunity to speak to a group of my peers by the company's owners regarding winning.

You Are Not Smaller Than the Room

This topic seemed appropriate for my life as I had lived almost my entire life focused on winning—games, academics, etc.

When I was asked to speak at the end of a general meeting about winning, I knew the opportunity was right for me. I took it very seriously and spoke to a room full of my peers— some had been in the company longer than I had, which could have made the situation a bit uncomfortable if I had allowed it.

I didn't let the idea of veteran agents in the same room discourage me. I was confident in my speaking abilities thanks in large part to my father who instilled in me the power of public speaking at an early age. I knew I could bring zeal and fire to the talk. This confidence helped propel not only myself but also others in the agency to believe that they *can* do really great things during what we called Win Week.

During a time when I'm trying to bring forth the winning culture that my environment brought to me growing up (such as during my talk to my company), I reflect on a time in 2005 when I got the opportunity to watch Taft University basketball team play in a championship game.

Their mantra all year long had been, "Losing is not an option."

I brought that message to my company that day during my speech.

I challenged others to set a goal, and not only just that but to do something that they had never done before. That was what winning was all about—going for something that you'd never achieved before and making strides toward making those dreams and goals your reality.

The goal that I set for myself during that time was a very specific number of sales for Win Week. I wanted to hit $10,000 in sales in one week. Sounds like a lofty goal, right? But I knew that in order to keep the winning culture alive within myself, I had to set a goal that I had never achieved.

While I knew this was probably a very ambitious goal to go after, I also knew that a man by the name of Ronald Rivera had hit $19,000 in sales in just one week.

Of course I felt a bit overwhelmed by the idea that I was coming in as practically a brand new person trying to hit a goal that was similar to a veteran agent's accomplishment. Had I not had the winning culture mindset, I might have thought I was too green to achieve the same thing.

But I chose to reframe that mindset and look at it from a different angle.

I viewed Ronald as a man who puts on his pants one leg at a time the same way that I do every single day. I knew that he had the same twenty-four hours in his day as I did in mine. **The only thing that separated him from me was his experience.**

Aside from that, I knew I could achieve at least $10,000 a week. So, I got in front of the room, spoke about what a winning culture looked like and how losing was not an option and created insane accountability for myself. When you are forced to say something such as your big, scary goal in front of a group of your peers, you feel the push and drive to back it up because you've already decided to talk the talk. Showtime begins when you have to walk the walk.

I was able to hit more than $10,000 in sales that week, and I certainly counted it as a win because I believed that losing was not an option for me. I knew that I had to do what my team needed me to do and that I owed it to myself at that point to get it done.

Holding yourself accountable and believing in yourself will align you with the winning culture and force you to be a winner later on in so many different areas of your life.

Chapter 5

Losing and Gaining Confidence

Confidence is one of those things that you can see in a person before words are even spoken.

I've been honored to have the opportunity to be around some incredibly confident people in my life. Their confidence and competence became something that I immediately took on within myself, and I started to embody the confidence that I was being exposed to.

One person who immediately comes to mind is my late Uncle Raymond - a mentor to my father who became my uncle by connection rather than by blood.

Raymond served as a positive male figure in my life during my childhood. He was there when I was born all the way through my college years. I fondly remember times when I was very young where Raymond swooped in to be the support system that I needed. If you remember from earlier in the book, Raymond was my go-to support for my preschool basketball game. That was the kind of unconditional love and support Raymond brought to my life, no matter how "silly" it may have seemed at the time.

What brings Raymond to mind when I think of confidence was the natural air that he had about him. He moved through a room and shook hands with everyone with his chest held high and a larger-than-life laugh.

That daily display of confidence showed me what it meant to be confident in public. But Uncle Raymond did more than just show me confidence. He talked a great deal about what it meant to be truly confident when we were not in public.

He spent time teaching me that I was just as important as everyone else and that nobody was any better than I was in this world. All the shortcomings in the world didn't stop me from being great. What did separate me from others was my confidence.

If you think back on your life, you may be able to pinpoint someone you've been close with or encountered that had a list of shortcomings they could've used as excuses for why they couldn't be as great as someone else. Instead of racking up the excuses, they decided to use their confidence to bring something positive to the room, even if the positivity was simply bringing a smile to someone's face or making them laugh out loud.

That is what makes a person feel confident in themselves - knowing what they bring to the table from the very beginning that makes others want to be around them, too.

Uncle Raymond always reiterated this idea and impressed upon the importance of this mindset. He made sure to tell me that if people wanted to be around someone else, they were doing something right.

He was also quick to say that this would only come to fruition if you are confident and believe in yourself from the start. You must be sure of your competency and know that everyone in the room should appreciate you being there simply by being you.

Learning these lessons about confidence has allowed me to build a foundation for myself full of confidence and competency. Even to this day, if I'm around a room full of people who are high net worth of millions or billions of dollars, I still believe that when I walk into that room, I'm there to enlighten another person.

Once you are able to truly embrace this mindset, your confidence will shoot through the roof.

Another person who comes to mind when I think about confidence is my dad.

While socioeconomics were not in my dad's favor growing up, he did have a loving home with parents who expressed their love for him often.

What my father and Uncle Raymond have in common is the fact that their families believed in them. They told my dad and Uncle Raymond that they could have anything they wanted in life. And that is what I believe, as well.

Now that I have a son of my own, I feel that it is my job to implore that upon my son now. I want him to know that he must walk with a certain swagger and believe in himself no matter what he must face throughout his life. Obstacles and faceless things in life must be run straight through without hesitation.

My dad always told me that if I wasn't good at something, I needed to work and work at it until I became more competent in that area. And this is something that you can instill in your life starting now.

The thing is, we all face difficulties. My son, for example, has struggled with reading for some time. And while I want him to have fun playing outside and experience the joys of childhood, I also want him to continue practicing the things he is not good at.

If you find yourself trying to do something that is a bit more difficult for you, or if you have a child who struggles in a certain area, remember that nothing gets better if it's not practiced. Everything that we do in life isn't going to be fun, but that doesn't mean it isn't something you shouldn't spend time on trying to improve.

When you work at getting better at something, you will see results. Sometimes these results are slow and steady, so take comfort in knowing that they *will* come if you continue to try. As the results start rolling in, your confidence will increase, too.

But there are times when losing confidence occurs. And there are a few different reasons I believe this happens.

1. We lose confidence because we do not know how to stand up and defend ourselves.

    When others say that you are not good enough at something, you may start to believe you don't deserve certain achievements or certain jobs. When we aren't able to fully stand up for ourselves and defend our competency, we lose the confidence that we did have.

2. We may lose confidence when our social status changes.

    For example, a divorce or a break up may cause us to lose confidence. Those types of social status changes tend to leave us wondering if we're not worth happiness or companionship. We may also allow negativity to creep into our lives because we think people are talking badly about us. Maybe you find yourself feeling less important in roles at your job due to changes. You may start questioning your competency and wondering why you can't be at the level of the person beside you.

3. We allow our financial situation to determine our confidence level and self-worth.

   Unfortunately, there are more people than not who allow financial status to make or break their confidence. Finances tend to leave us feeling like we're not enough and can't do enough based on the financial situation we're currently in. Limitations and restrictions can cause people to lose confidence when others around them are not facing the same issues.

Equating your self-worth and value to your financial situation can be detrimental to your confidence and mindset. Luckily, you can absolutely bring that confidence back.

Bringing back lost confidence doesn't require any elaborate schemes or spending a great deal of money on yourself.

In fact, getting your confidence back can be achieved by spending time in self-actualization and remembering all the great things that others see in you. Getting a better perspective on how you see yourself and how others truly view what you bring to the table can being your self-worth back to where it belongs.

I once read a book by Marshall Goldsmith, *MOJO,* who wrote about how to get confidence, how to keep it, and how to get it back if you lose it.

One of the main points that Goldsmith spoke about in his book was that in order to bring back lost confidence, one had to spend quality time with themselves.

If you can't spend time with yourself reflecting and remembering all the amazing things about you, who else is going to appreciate you? The big thing here is once you lose confidence, you have to realize what it is you have lost before you can get it back. And the way to do that is by spending time with yourself.

You can also spend time around other confident people to help you start putting in place some different measurables that may stretch you a little bit on the confidence scale. Being around other confident people will certainly build your foundation to a level that you need it to be in order to feel fully confident and competent.

From there, start interacting with other situations that may make you feel a little bit more uncomfortable, but that are going to help you build your confidence a little bit more. For example, when you start to then realize that you can lift weights, you can move on to boxing classes. While these activities may seem rather different, they both require you to use your body strength. When you are able to accomplish one thing, you can move on to something that requires the same skills you've already mastered in order to become proficient at another skill.

When you are able to use the skills and competency it took to achieve one thing, you can use that confidence in other areas along your journey that can be implemented in other areas throughout your life.

Remember that confidence is never truly lost. All you must do is take time to find it again.

Chapter 6

Fear of the Unknown

As we discussed in the previous chapter, losing confidence does happen. It may occur intermittently throughout our lives, but the one thing that remains is it is never lost for good.

When people begin to lose confidence, it typically means they have a lack of information for what's to come. The fear of the unknown can be crippling for some people, especially as it relates to their confidence.

Heading into new situations without knowledge of what's to come can be damaging to our confidence. It's easier to lose confidence when we have no control over the situation. That confidence we once had may recede because it's easier to tell yourself you're just not good enough for whatever comes your way.

It's important to remember that **everyone starts at ground zero** in almost every situation. Those people that have made it big are those who trusted the process and let go of control. They are the ones who allowed the idea that real life is full of struggles. Anything worth having is worth fighting for. And that may be exactly what you face when you enter into a new situation. But letting the fear of what *could* happen keep you from going for it and lacking confidence in your ability to achieve your goal is simply going to continue to hold you back from greatness.

Brendon Burchard says it best with his tagline, "Honor the struggle."

We have to really go back and reflect on past situations that required us to take a leap of faith and trust our confidence and competency. What was hard at that the time didn't kill us; therefore, we can successfully make it through the next obstacle.

Through confidence, we must realize that we've achieved great things. Understanding that we are worth it - the struggles, the hardships, the obstacles - will allow us to fully reach all the various goals we have set for our self.

In the sales world, we tend to lose confidence all the time, especially when it relates to direct sales. Unfortunately, the weight of making the sales goal for the week, month, or quarter can be daunting for some.

I've seen it and experienced it personally. If a person does not have the confidence and doesn't trust himself or herself fully, it is very easy to slip down a slippery slope into a place where everything looks like a negative.

My mentor once told me that we're all going to have ups and downs in life. The key to staying on the path toward achieving your goals is to see those low periods in your life more like molehills rather than massive mountains and drop-offs.

There was a particular time in my life that I remember going through a drought in the sales world that forced me to believe I wasn't good enough. Things weren't falling the way they normally did, and it was bringing me way down.

I took some time to really reflect on the situation in order to find out what was happening. The thing was, everything was on point. I was using my normal script to speak with potential buyers, the rest of the process was running as it should, but I wasn't making sales.

What I eventually realized was that sometimes there will be a little bit of a lull in this sales world, and not every day can be an exceptional day. Sometimes, the problem isn't *you*. Sometimes the problem is someone else or outside circumstances out of your control.

Of course, in order to figure that out, one must truly self-reflect. As long as you're doing that, whatever conclusion you come to regarding the issue will be the answer.

Take a look at yourself in the mirror first before deciding what the problem is. If you have the confidence in yourself to say that you have done your best, and times are just a little bit more difficult at the moment, then that's all it is.

One thing we tend to not plan for, especially in the sales world, is the trapdoor. That safety net or backup plan.

If you don't have an alternative option when your original plan doesn't work, you may find it more difficult to move forward. But, if you can understand that you're still okay, and all you need to do is use the confidence you already have to keep forging forward, you will be just fine.

Creating a foundation for yourself with a backup plan in the instance that life throws you a few curve balls will certainly leave your confidence less shaken in the long run. When you're not stressing yourself out based off ideas and desires, you can create additional plans that allow you to put in place action steps to get you to your original goal in the end.

Finding yourself in a bit of a rough patch may require you to step out into the unknown and face the fears you may have been avoiding. Get back to the fundamentals of why you wanted to go for the goal in the first place. Break it down for yourself and look at the pieces to the big puzzle.

Let's look at direct sales for example.

In direct sales, you must remember your script and what/how you're selling your product. What are the key components for making the sale? What are the positives, and how can you be a liaison for your product?

Breaking down the key pieces to getting the goal achieved is what will help you gain confidence that you may have lost due to the fear of the unknown. When you're able to see what you bring to the table, you are then able to gain the confidence you need to push through the fear and get to your desired destination.

Ask yourself some questions like:

1. What is it that I bring to this relationship?
2. How am I going to help this person who's across from me?
3. How am I going to help this person increase their worth?
4. What is that person going to get from me?

When we are able to take time and do self-reflection, we will inevitably boost our confidence. Knowing what our baseline, our foundation, for what it is we can do for the situation will help us to see the positives rather than the negatives when it comes to what we bring to the forefront.

Surrounding Ourselves with Others

It's quite possible that the fear of the unknown causes some of us to retreat to places that don't require interaction with other people.

For example, confidence comes when we know that we're going to be okay, or that we can do whatever it is we need to do well.

But when the unknown scares us enough to keep us locked away from the outside world, we can never increase our confidence.

The thing is, you are NOT smaller than the room. In fact, you are sitting in your home that is safe to you but won't help you in the long run. You may accomplish small goals, but in the grand scheme of things, you won't be able to become the person you truly want to be within your family and relationships with other people.

There have been quite a few times in my life where staying in the comfort of my own home would have been much more enjoyable than facing my fears and testing the waters. And that may be something you have faced or are currently facing in your life.

What I like to do is look directly at the day and decide who needs me. It may be that someone at work in my family needs me to be the best that I can be that day for various reasons, but I can't be that person if I'm afraid.

Sure, you may find yourself in a room full of people who have accomplished great things, who are where you want to be, and who you know may have accomplished things that are bigger than you ever dreamed. But the important thing to remember is that you can be the best you in your little room, but being the best you in the bigger room is much more important.

Remind yourself that you *can* bring influence and change to the room if you show up. But when you choose to stay hidden because you're afraid, nothing can happen.

Take yourself out of the twelve-foot space and allow yourself to be uncomfortable for a minute. **That feeling of discomfort will bring you greater confidence down the road.** All you have to tell yourself is that you are *not* smaller than any room you step into.

Feeling confident when you're by yourself can translate into being confident when you're with other people. Pull from others around you that have the confidence you want and show yourself that the knowledge you have and the skills you have acquired will take you further than you ever imagined.

Chapter 7

Socioeconomics and Confidence

Socioeconomics is something that is looked at in many different areas of our world today. You find schools across the country analyzing socioeconomics to determine curriculum. You find companies using socioeconomics to create products and services for certain areas of the country.

Whatever socioeconomics is used for, many great things come from this information.

Socioeconomic status can make or break a person's confidence from the start.

Let's take a look at those who are in lower socioeconomic status.

This group of the population tends to find themselves caught up in the horrible cycle of not seeing confidence, therefore not gaining confidence.

Maybe no one believed in their lofty dreams or desires. Maybe no one told them that they could eventually get where they wanted to go one day. This lack of confidence in either the support system around them or in themselves creates a vicious cycle that perpetuates low self-esteem and lack of confidence.

However, luckily for them, there are those people who are the exceptions to the rules. There are people who live within the low socioeconomic status who break the mold and live out of the mold. They aspire to do greater things because they believe they can! That belief may come from one great influence in their life or from within themselves.

Either way, their confidence stems from parents who refuse to let their children experience the same hardships they experienced simply because their financial situation is less than ideal. These are the people whose parents told them they could do whatever they wanted, be whoever they wanted to be, and do more than they ever dreamed.

Those are the kids who find a way, who work hard to achieve something, and who use their competency to create confidence within themselves. You may see these kids on the playground, walking with their chest puffed out acting, as leaders in the sand, and leading others to greatness regardless of what their finances are.

However, on the flip side, you have those who aren't very confident because of their socioeconomic status and refuse to break the cycle. Instead, they bring others down with them because that is all they know. They have someone around them who is succeeding, but they'd rather pull them down with them to their level instead of rising to the occasion and being more like the person who is succeeding. We call this the two crabs in a barrel situation.

It's safe to say that there is a middle group among both extremes. This group is made up of those who have an unfortunate socioeconomic status, that want to do better and have the support to get them there.

These are the people that know they're worth more than they're currently experiencing and can do more than they're currently doing.

Growing up in Central Los Angeles, I happened to be one of those middle group kids who had all the support from my family and was exposed to a wide variety of different things. My support system showed me that the sky was truly the limit and anything I ever wanted in life I could get based off my own merit.

Inside of my soul, I knew with 100% certainty that it was true about getting things I wanted based on my own merit because of the support system I was blessed with in my life.

When I transitioned into a completely new career field (direct sales), I had never been in this industry before. It was a scary leap, but taking it to the next level and telling myself that I knew people who were successful in the field and that I could be, too. I wasn't willing to let my childhood socioeconomic status determine how successful I was as an adult.

That attitude is crucial to being successful in the world today. Your attitude may not always reflect this belief—we're only human, but having a strong foundation with that mindset at the core could mean the difference between failure and success.

If you find yourself struggling to get out of the mindset that you can't be successful because of how you grew up, remember this: **those people who have hit it big are doing the exact same things you're doing every day.** They're eating breakfast, putting on their clothes, and going to sleep at night the exact same way you do.

What you must be willing to do is put yourself out there and get a plan in place to elevate yourself to those next levels you want to achieve.

If you had a tougher upbringing—financially or family dynamics or both—you may be able to utilize those experiences to make you a stronger, more confident person as an adult. Think about it this way: you are already aware that everything isn't roses and sunshine. Sometimes growing up in a concrete jungle or a rural area can give insight as to how to push through difficult situations others may not fully understand.

Having a rough start may also give you more perspective on what you're doing and who you're doing it for. There are most likely people in your life that you want to make proud, and that is something that stands true for anyone who propelled themselves forward and out of those lower economic situations to make a better life for themselves.

Then, there are those people who come from completely different worlds and still struggle with confidence.

Those are the people who grow up with affluence. It would seem that those who grew up with everything at their fingertips, ranging from finances to support systems, would find it easier to feel positive and confident about themselves. This is not always the case.

Let's examine a brother and sister situation.

The sister may be the one who took everything from the parents and fully invested her life into building a foundation based on the values and ideas her parents instilled in her as a child. She may have watched how her parents gave her the lifestyle she had because they were able to and wanted to see her be successful. Now, she's working a fulltime job and doing great things because she understands that the sky's the limit. She is making her parents proud day in and day out.

She had confidence in her abilities because her mom and dad taught her to walk a certain way and hold her shoulders back, head up high, and that goes a very long way.

The brother went off on the complete opposite side of the scale. He felt an insane amount of pressure from his parents to do great things and be successful in business, in the community, and in life in general. The affluence he had was something he couldn't live up to. The shoes were too big to fill, and he felt as if he wasn't good enough to do what needed to be done. Instead, he decided to become a couch potato and live off his mom and dad for as long he could. The comfort he had created for himself was what kept him unconfident and incapable of forging forward to pave a better way for himself.

As a parent, how does one go about fixing that problem, especially when it's so personal?

The answer is to work very hard on yourself first. No one can make you want to do something, and **confidence cannot be forced upon anyone.**

If you want to remedy the issue for yourself, you must sit back and evaluate what has been happening in your life leading up to the point you're at now. As an adult, it may be harder to get out of your set ways, but there has to be a moment in your life that makes you realize what you're doing isn't working any longer. Something must be done in order to live a happy and fulfilled life, and the current situation isn't doing that for you.

When you experience that awakening where your real life isn't enough anymore, you will be able to fully embrace the fact that the people who love and support you wanted nothing more than to give you what you needed to succeed on your own.

Confidence must be something you work on daily. You have to truly believe that you can do and be more than whatever your current position is. The most important thing is you cannot give up on yourself because other people haven't.

No matter how much skill or competency you possess in this world, a lack of confidence can shoot all of it down in a second. There may be other people around you currently who are doing better than you are—they're successful, happy, living on their own, raising families, or chasing their dreams. So, in order for you to meet them there, you have to desire to be competent and skilled in something in order to increase your confidence to that kind of level.

The intrinsic desire, the one deep down in your soul, is what will move you forward. It does not matter one bit what the outside says. What matters is that you are living through the moment and know what you need to feel in order to make things happen.

You may find that one day the switch just flips—you're feeling ready to go and ready to get through the fire to the other side.

There is a fire inside of you already. The question is: are you ready to get past whatever upbringing has created this story *for* you and start creating your own story for yourself?

Chapter 8

Self-Love: The Foundation

Self-love is quite the buzzword in today's world, with so many people using it to describe taking care of themselves with manicures, massages, or even lunch dates with friends.

But what exactly *is* self-love? **Self-love is the foundation of which we build appreciation for ourselves upon.** Self-love is reminding yourself that you're awesome, smart, funny, and loved by many. It is also understanding you're living a good life, working hard, and doing the things that need to be done in order to give you the life you want.

How does self-love relate to confidence?

People who are the most confident are those who are in love with themselves first and foremost. This isn't referring to the narcissistic love that some people have for themselves, but rather the type of self-love that allows your entire being to be content with who you are and what you've accomplished throughout your lifetime. This type of love also includes being comfortable with what others may or may not think about you and giving yourself the room to grow and do what's best for you despite other's opinions.

Of course, having a healthy relationship with ourselves shouldn't involve worrying too much about what others think of us, but we do need to keep in mind that perception is everything. How we perceive things or how others perceive us is what plays a major part in our self-love as well as the image that we see ourselves in on a regular basis.

You Are Not Smaller Than the Room

One way you can truly fall in love with yourself and increase your confidence is to be fully in tune with your why. The main thing that is going to propel your success and confidence forward is being in tune with why you're doing what you're doing, and why it is so important to you.

I am fully aware of my why. Have I always been confident in *why* I want to do what I do both as a businessman and a father? No. But now that I am in tune with my why, I feel confident in my abilities to achieve great success.

My why is simply this: I want to be successful enough that my son can say he is proud of his dad for being a hard worker. I'm also doing this so that he can see what a great role model looks like that works hard and gets done what needs to be done through perseverance and dedication.

As any father does, I want great things for my son. I want him to know that great things are coming for him. My job is to emulate a positive model of what can come from a person working hard and achieving success at high levels regardless of what life throws their way. If I want my son to see me as successful and never a failure, I cannot give myself the option to fail. Once he sees that in me, he will believe it.

Understanding my why has helped me to truly practice self-love, and you can, too.

When we are in tune with our why, it is easier to remember things that are important to us on a day to day basis. Although we may find ourselves getting sucked into the mundane tasks that come with our jobs, we must always remember that our why is bigger than just work. Our why is what keeps us going and keeps the fire burning inside of ourselves.

It's okay if you don't want to sit down and do the videos or plan what needs to come next. The fear of missing out on the fun things in life is a real fear, but it doesn't have to stay that way. You can choose to remember that sometimes you have to work hard to see the good days.

Using our self-love and our why to help us see that something bigger is always pushing us can help us see what really matters in our lives.

Being in tune with your why boosts your confidence to great heights. How? Well, when I started working at my current job, I was very green. I had never truly been in sales before, but I had experience in recruiting. That experience helped me become a better salesperson because I was able to see what it took to get people to commit to you—whether it involved playing for me on my team or purchasing a product from my company.

I was confident that I could use my experience of bringing people onto my basketball team to help bring others into a company that I believed in.

In February of 2016, when I took the job as a life insurance salesperson, I knew one thing: the first thing that goes along with sales is confidence. A wise man by the name of Grant Cardone once said these words, and he couldn't have been more right. He also said that we must always remember we are *that* person—whoever you are in business, whoever you are in life, you are *that* person!

Knowing this confidently allows you to do something that may be out of your league or comfort zone. Even though I had played sports all my life, trying something new in the insurance field felt right because of the self-love I had for myself and the understanding of my skills that I brought to whatever environment I was in.

There may be times when your self-love and confidence are tested. This is completely normal. In fact, it might be quite worrisome if you didn't experience moments of doubt along the way. It's human nature.

Having your why tested can feel slightly discouraging. You may be struggling to figure out if what you're doing is the right thing, or whether or not you have the skills to be successful in a particular position. I learned that when a person has all the intangibles, such as the ability to speak to people fluently, or the ability to educate potential clients about their next best steps, that is what keeps a person's why burning.

If you find yourself struggling to fully believe in yourself and love yourself from within, create reminders for yourself in your cell phone. Let those reminders pop up throughout the day and tell you that you're loved by lots, you are an influential person, and you have the ability to be liked by those in the room. These are the affirmations that will build that confidence for you when you know that you're entering a new, scary situation (or any situation, really).

These affirmations can make or break your entire day.

It is crucial that you remind yourself of past accomplishments because they will be the moments that give you the boost because you know you've already successfully done it in the past.

Those self-reminders help us increase our self-love which then increases our confidence.

Confidence can be a tricky thing in life, but it doesn't have to be.

Struggling with a lack of confidence or feeling like you're much smaller than the room is over. It's time to fully embrace the idea that you *can* because you *are*.

It really is that simple.

You *can* do something because you *are* you. That's all you need to know.

You can go to the next level because it's all just a building block and pulling from different portions of confidence that you've gathered over the years to create a whole person (you) who believes in yourself and your abilities to achieve greatness.

There is no doubt that you *are* bigger than any room you ever step foot and regardless of who you're surrounded by in that room.

You are **confident.** You are a **star.**

About the Author

Temesghen Starr lives a life where the glass is half full in all occasions. A native of Los Angeles, he currently resides in Southern California and is a regional manager for American Income Life. Industry changes have helped him to create a platform that promotes self-confidence. Most recently he spent time as the director of development for athletics at the Montana State University Foundation.

Prior to a stint at the foundation, he had a tenure at Montana State University as assistant coach for the men's basketball team. Starr also had a stop in Marshalltown, Iowa in the same position. He started his career coaching and teaching others at high-school level at South Bay Lutheran and Taft High-School. This time catapulted the efforts of developing and leading others in their efforts to greatness.

www.linkedin.com/in/temesghen-starr-846b0148/
https://www.instagram.com/temesghenstarr/
https://twitter.com/temesghenstarr

CPSIA information can be obtained
at www.ICGtesting.com
Printed in the USA
FSHW022145221218
54416FS